Guide for Developing High-Quality Emergency Operations Plans for Houses of Worship

June 2013

Table of Contents

This page intentionally left blank.

Introduction and Purpose

Many people think of a house of worship as a safe area where violence and emergencies cannot affect them. However, violence in houses of worship is not a new phenomenon. In addition to violent acts, fires, tornadoes, floods, hurricanes, earthquakes, and arson also affect houses of worship. With many incidents occurring with little to no warning, many houses of worship are developing and updating plans and procedures to ensure the safety and security of their congregations, staff, and facilities.

In collaboration with other houses of worship and community partners (i.e., governmental entities that have a responsibility in the plan, including first responders, public health officials, and mental health officials), houses of worship can take steps to plan for these potential emergencies through the creation of an emergency operations plan (EOP). Additionally, community organizations and private sector entities may have a role in the plan. Houses of worship are distinctive settings in that congregants share a common bond and have a predisposition to volunteer. The demographics of a congregation often mean that children and the elderly are present and may need assistance.

This guide provides houses of worship with information regarding emergency operations planning for the spectrum of threats and hazards they may face. It discusses actions that may be taken before, during, and after an incident in order to reduce the impact on property and any loss of life and it encourages every house of worship to develop an EOP.

The Departments issuing this guidance are providing examples of good practices and matters to consider for planning and implementation purposes. The guidance does not create any requirements beyond those included in applicable law and regulations, or create any additional rights for any person, entity, or organization. Moreover, the Departments fully understand that congregations may approach some of these issues differently than government and other community organizations. At the same time, the Departments would like to assist congregations that are interested in emergency operations planning, and this guidance is offered in that spirit. The information presented in this document generally constitutes informal guidance and provides examples that may be helpful. The inclusion of certain references does not imply any endorsement of any documents, products, or approaches. Other resources may be equally helpful.

It is recommended that planning teams responsible for developing and revising a house of worship's EOP use this document to guide their efforts. To gain the most from this guide, users should read the entire document prior to initiating their planning efforts and refer back to it throughout the planning process.[1] The guide is organized in four sections:

- The principles of emergency operations planning

- A process for developing, implementing, and continually refining a house of worship's EOP with community partners

- A discussion of the form and function of a house of worship's EOP

---

[1] All Web sites listed in this guide were accessible as of June 6, 2013.

- A closer look that discusses house of worship emergency planning in the event of an active shooter situation.

This guide is designed to be scalable for use by small to large-sized houses of worship in order to help navigate the planning process. Used in its entirety, this guide provides information on the fundamentals of planning and their application. At a minimum, houses of worship are encouraged to complete the planning process and develop a basic plan. This guide does not impose any new Federal requirements. While some Federal requirements may apply to houses of worship that receive Federal funding, they are not addressed in this document. For houses of worship that also operate a school, please see the *Guide for Developing High-quality School Emergency Operations Plans* for planning considerations specific to the school environment.[2]

Emergency planning efforts work best when they are aligned with emergency planning practices at the local, state, and national levels. Recent developments have put a new emphasis on the process for developing EOPs. National preparedness efforts, including planning, are informed by Presidential Policy Directive (PPD) 8, which was signed by the President in March of 2011 and describes the Nation's approach to preparedness. This Directive represents an evolution in our collective understanding of national preparedness, based on the lessons learned from criminal activities, hurricanes, house of worship incidents, and other experiences.

PPD-8 defines preparedness around five mission areas: Prevention, Protection, Mitigation, Response, and Recovery.

- **Prevention**, for the purposes of this guide, means the capabilities necessary to avoid, deter, or stop an imminent crime or threatened or actual mass casualty incident.[3] Prevention is the action houses of worship take to prevent a threatened or actual incident from occurring.

- **Protection** means the capabilities to secure houses of worship against acts of terrorism and manmade or natural disasters. Protection focuses on ongoing actions that protect people, networks, and property from a threat or hazard.

- **Mitigation** means the capabilities necessary to eliminate or reduce the loss of life and property damage by lessening the impact of an incident. In this guide, mitigation also means reducing the likelihood that threats and hazards will happen.

- **Response** means the capabilities necessary to stabilize an incident once it has already happened or is certain to happen in an unpreventable way; establish a safe and secure environment; save lives and property; and facilitate the transition to recovery.

- **Recovery** means the capabilities necessary to assist houses of worship affected by an incident in restoring their environment.

Emergency management officials and emergency responders engaging with houses of worship are familiar with this terminology. These mission areas generally align with the three timeframes associated with an incident: before, during, and after. The majority of Prevention, Protection, and Mitigation activities generally occur before an incident, although these three mission areas do

---

[2] U.S. Department of Education, et al. 2013. *Guide for Developing High-quality School Emergency Operations Plans*. Washington, DC: U.S. Department of Education. http://rems.ed.gov

[3] In the broader PPD-8 construct, the term "prevention" refers to those capabilities necessary to avoid, prevent, or stop a threatened or actual act of terrorism. The term "prevention" refers to preventing imminent threats.

have ongoing activities that can occur throughout the incident. Response activities occur during an incident and Recovery activities can begin during an incident and occur after an incident. To help avoid confusion over terms and allow for ease of reference, this guide uses the terms *before*, *during*, and *after*.

As houses of worship plan for and execute response and recovery activities through the EOP, they should consider using the concepts and principles of the National Incident Management System (NIMS). NIMS provides all those involved with a common understanding of roles and responsibilities during response to incidents. Houses of worship may also find NIMS suitable for managing other large-scale non-emergency events, such as fairs or festivals. One component of NIMS is the Incident Command System (ICS), which provides a standardized approach for incident management, regardless of cause, size, location, or complexity. By using ICS during an incident, houses of worship will be able to work more effectively with the responders in their community.[4]

While some of the vocabulary, processes and approaches discussed in this guide may be new to congregations, they are critical to the creation of emergency management practices and plans that are integrated with the efforts of first responders (e.g., fire, law enforcement, emergency medical services [EMS]) and other key stakeholders. If a house of worship has an existing plan, revising and adapting that plan using the principles and process described in this guide will help ensure alignment with the terminology and approaches used across the Nation, including the first responders with whom the house of worship will need to collaborate before, during, and after an incident.

Planning Principles

The following principles are key to developing a house of worship EOP that addresses a range of threats and hazards.

- **Planning should be supported by leadership.** The leadership of the house of worship should initiate and support planning efforts to ensure engagement from the congregation and outreach to the entire community. Regardless of the size of the house of worship, one or more persons should lead emergency planning efforts.

- **Planning considers all threats and hazards.** The planning process should take into account a wide range of possible threats and hazards that may affect the house of worship. Emergency operations planning considers all threats and hazards throughout the planning process, addressing safety needs before, during, and after an incident.

- **Planning considers all setting and all times.** It is important to remember that threats and hazards can affect the house of worship at non-standard times (e.g., when facilities are being used by others), as well as off-site (e.g., an activity or event sponsored somewhere other than the grounds of the house of worship).

- **Planning provides for the access and functional needs of the whole house of worship community.** The whole house of worship community includes regular attendees, guests, and staff, including those with disabilities and others with access and functional needs; those

---

[4] For more information on NIMS and ICS, please see http://www.fema.gov/national-incident-management-system.

from racially and ethnically diverse backgrounds; and people with limited English proficiency.

▪ **A model EOP is created by following a collaborative process.** This guide provides a process, plan format, and content guidance that is flexible enough for use by all house of worship emergency planning teams. If the planning team also uses templates, it should take steps to first evaluate their usefulness to ensure the tools do not undermine the collaborative initiative and collectively shared plan. There are some jurisdictions that provide templates and these will reflect local and state mandates, as applicable.

The Planning Process

There are many ways to develop a plan. The planning process discussed in this section is flexible and can be adapted to accommodate a house of worship's unique characteristics and situation. Effective emergency operations planning is not done in isolation. It is critical that houses of worship work with their local emergency management agency and community partners, including first responders, during the planning process, as an effective house of worship EOP is integrated with community, regional, and state plans. This collaboration makes more resources available and helps to ensure the seamless integration of all responders.

Figure 1 depicts the six steps in the planning process.[5] At each step in the planning process, houses of worship should consider the impact of their decisions on ongoing activities such as training and exercises, as well as on equipment and resources.

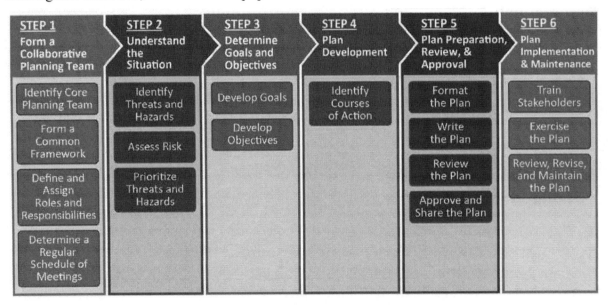

Figure 1: Steps in the Planning Process

---

[5] For more information, please see *Developing and Maintaining Emergency Operations Plans (Comprehensive Preparedness Guide [CPG] 101), Version 2.0* (Federal Emergency Management Agency, 2011, http://www.fema.gov/plan).

Step 1: Form a Collaborative Planning Team

Experience and lessons learned indicate that operational planning is best performed by a team. Case studies reinforce this concept by pointing out that the common thread found in successful operations is that participating organizations have understood and accepted their roles. Close collaboration between houses of worship and community partners, including first responders, ensures the coordination of efforts and the integration of plans. Houses of worship may consider joining or collaborating with other nearby houses of worship to form joint emergency planning teams. In addition, first responders and emergency managers may want to work with multiple houses of worship to address common goals and objectives.

Identify Core Planning Team

The core planning team should include representatives from the house of worship, as well as first responders and others who may have roles and responsibilities in house of worship emergency management before, during, and after an incident. Many houses of worship may have first responders or others with special emergency planning expertise in their congregation. Their expertise will inform the development, implementation, and refinement of the house of worship's plan. Where possible, consider including diverse representation on the planning team, including individuals with disabilities and the elderly. The planning team should be small enough to permit close collaboration, yet large enough to be representative of the house of worship, its congregation, and its community partners. It should also be large enough as to not place an undue burden on any single person.

Form a Common Framework

All team members should consider taking time to learn each other's vocabulary, command structure, and culture in order to facilitate effective planning.

Define and Assign Roles and Responsibilities

Each person involved in the development and refinement of the plan should know his or her role and responsibility in the planning process, as well as generally understand others' roles so that they know with whom to speak regarding particular issues and questions that might arise during the planning process.

Determine a Regular Schedule of Meetings

Regularly scheduled planning meetings reinforce the ongoing planning effort. Establishing a flexible but regular schedule of meeting times will facilitate greater collaboration, coordination, and communication among team members and will help solidify crucial relationships.

Step 1 Outcome

After completing Step 1, the house of worship will have formed a planning team with representation from all necessary stakeholders. The planning team will have taken initial steps to form a common framework; define and assign roles and responsibilities in the planning process; and set a schedule of planning meetings.

Step 2: Understand the Situation

In Step 2, the planning team identifies possible threats and hazards and assesses the risk and vulnerabilities posed by those threats and hazards. Effective emergency planning depends on an analysis and comparison of the threats and hazards a particular house of worship faces. This is typically performed through a threat and hazard identification and risk assessment process that collects information about threats and hazards and assigns values to risk for the purposes of deciding which threats and hazards the plan should prioritize and subsequently address.

Identify Threats and Hazards

The planning team first needs to understand the threats and hazards faced by the house of worship and the surrounding community. The planning team can draw upon a wealth of existing information to identify the range of threats and hazards that may be faced by the house of worship. First, the planning team members should share their own knowledge of threats and hazards the house of worship and surrounding community has faced in the past or may face in the future. Houses of worship should work with their local emergency management agency to obtain a copy of the state or local risk assessment. This assessment contains information regarding the potential threats and hazards in the community that may also affect the house of worship.

Assess the Risk Posed by Identified Threats and Hazards

Once an initial set of threats and hazards has been identified through the process described above, the planning team should select suitable assessment tools to evaluate the risk posed by the identified threats and hazards.[6] Evaluating risk involves understanding the probability that the specific threat or hazard will occur; the effects the threat or hazard will likely have, including their severity; the time the house of worship will have to warn occupants about the threat or hazard; and how long the threat or hazard may last.

The house of worship's local emergency management agency should be able to provide information on the threats and hazards identified for the surrounding community. This enables the planning team to focus its assessment efforts on threats and hazards unique to the house of worship, as well as the particular vulnerabilities of the buildings and their occupants.[7] Assessing risk and vulnerability enables the planning team to focus its efforts on prioritized threats and hazards.

A site assessment examines the safety, accessibility, and emergency preparedness of the house of worship's buildings and grounds. This assessment includes, but is not limited to, a review of building access; visibility around the exterior of buildings; structural integrity of buildings; compliance with applicable architectural standards for individuals with disabilities and others with access and functional needs; and emergency vehicle access. The planning team may also identify additional threats and hazards through the site assessment process.

---

[6] For more information on the threat and hazard identification and risk assessment process, please see *Threat and Hazard Identification and Risk Assessment Guide (CPG 201)* (U.S. Department of Homeland Security [DHS], 2012, http://www.fema.gov/plan).

[7] "Vulnerabilities" are characteristics that could make the house of worship more susceptible to threats and hazards.

After conducting threat and hazard identification, the planning team should organize the information into a format that is useful for comparison of the risks posed by the identified threats and hazards. This information will then be used to assess and compare the threats and hazards and their likely consequences, commonly referred to as a risk assessment. One effective method for organizing information is create a table with information about each possible threat and hazard, including any new threats or hazards identified through the assessment process. The table should include:

- Probability or frequency of occurrence (i.e., how often it may occur)

- Magnitude (i.e., the extent of expected damage)

- Time available to warn occupants

- Duration (i.e., how long the threat or hazard will be occurring)

- Follow-on effects

Prioritize Threats and Hazards

The planning team should use the information it has organized to compare and prioritize risks posed by the threats and hazards. This will allow the team to decide which threats or hazards it will directly address in the plan. The team should consider multiple factors in order to develop an indicator of risk. One option is a mathematical approach, which assigns index numbers (e.g., 1-to-4 scale) for different categories of information used in the ranking scheme. Using this approach, the planning team can categorize threats and hazards as posing a relatively high, medium, or low risk. Table 1 provides an example risk assessment worksheet for comparing and prioritizing threats and hazards.

Table 1: Example Risk Assessment Worksheet

Hazard	Probability	Magnitude	Warning	Duration	Risk Priority
Earthquake	4. Highly Likely 3. Likely 2. Possible 1. Unlikely	4. Catastrophic 3. Critical 2. Limited 1. Negligible	4. Minimal 3. 6-12 Hours 2. 12-24 Hours 1. > 24 Hours	4. 12+ Hours 3. 6-12 Hours 2. 3-6 Hours 1. < 3 Hours	High Medium Low
Fire	4. Highly Likely 3. Likely 2. Possible 1. Unlikely	4. Catastrophic 3. Critical 2. Limited 1. Negligible	4. Minimal 3. 6-12 Hours 2. 12-24 Hours 1. > 24 Hours	4. 12+ Hours 3. 6-12 Hours 2. 3-6 Hours 1. < 3 Hours	High Medium Low

Step 2 Outcome

After completing Step 2, the planning team will have a prioritized (e.g., high, medium, or low risk) list of threats and hazards based on the results of the threat and hazard identification and risk assessment.

Step 3: Determine Goals and Objectives

In Step 3, the planning team decides which of the threats and hazards identified in Step 2 will be addressed in the house of worship's plan. The planning team may decide to address only those threats and hazards that were classified as high risk, or they may decide to address all threats and hazards classified as high risk, as well as some of the threats and hazards that were classified as medium risk. This is a critical decision point in the planning process. It is recommended that the planning team address more than only the high-risk threats and hazards.

Develop Goals and Objectives

Once the planning team has determined the threats and hazards that will be addressed in the plan, it should develop goals and objectives for each threat or hazard.

Goals are broad, general statements that indicate the desired outcome in response to a threat or hazard. Goals are what personnel and other resources are supposed to achieve. Goals also help identify when major activities are complete and what defines a successful outcome.

The planning team should develop at least three goals for addressing each threat or hazard (although the planning team may want to identify more). Those three goals should indicate the desired outcome for before, during, and after the threat or hazard.

> **Example: Goals for a Fire Hazard**
>
> Three possible goals for a fire hazard include:
>
> *Goal #1 (Before):* Prevent a fire from occurring in the house of worship.
>
> *Goal #2 (During):* Protect all persons and property from injury by the fire.
>
> *Goal #3 (After):* Provide necessary medical attention to those in need.

Objectives are specific, measurable actions that are necessary to achieve the goals. Often, planners will need to identify multiple objectives in support of a single goal.

> **Example: Objectives for a Fire Hazard**
>
> For Goal #1 in the fire hazard example, possible objectives include:
>
> - *Objective 1.1:* Provide fire prevention training to all persons that use combustible materials or equipment in or around the house of worship.
> - *Objective 1.2:* Store combustible materials in fireproof containers or rooms.
>
> For Goal #2 in the preceding example, possible objectives include:
>
> - *Objective 2.1:* Evacuate all persons from the building and surrounding grounds immediately.
> - *Objective 2.2:* Account for all persons known to be on site.
>
> For Goal #3 in the preceding example, possible objectives include:
>
> - *Objective 3.1:* Immediately notify 911, fire, and EMS of any fire in the house of worship.
> - *Objective 3.2:* Immediately begin to provide first aid.

After the planning team has developed the objectives for each goal, it will find that certain critical *functions* or activities apply to more than one threat or hazard. Examples of these crosscutting functions include evacuation, shelter-in-place, and lockdown. After identifying these functions, the planning team should develop three goals for each function. As with the goals already identified for threats and hazards, the three goals should indicate the desired outcome for before, during, and after the function has been executed. These commonly occurring functions will be contained in functional annexes to the plan.[8] More details on these functions are included in the "Plan Content" section of this guide, including issues to consider as goals and objectives are developed for these functions. Once the goals for a function are identified, possible supporting objectives are identified.

Example: Goals and Objectives for an Evacuation Function

For an evacuation function, three possible goals and associated objectives include:

Function Goal Example 1 (Before): Ensure all persons know their evacuation route.

- *Objective 1.1:* Assess, identify, and communicate the location of assembly points to be used during an evacuation.

Function Goal Example 2 (During): Evacuate the house of worship immediately.

- *Objective 2.1:* All persons will evacuate the house of worship using assigned routes.

Function Goal Example 3 (After): Confirm that all persons have left the building.

- *Objective 3.1:* Safely sweep the building.

Step 3 Outcome

After completing Step 3, the planning team will have at least three goals for each threat or hazard and function, as well as objectives for each goal.

Step 4: Plan Development (Identifying Courses of Action)

In Step 4, the planning team develops courses of action for accomplishing each of the objectives identified in Step 3 (for threats, hazards, and functions). Courses of action address the what/who/when/where/why/how for each threat or hazard and function. The planning team should examine each course of action to determine whether it is feasible and whether the stakeholders necessary to implement it find it acceptable. For additional considerations for developing courses of action, please see the "Plan Content" section of this guide.

Courses of action include criteria for determining how and when each response will be implemented under a variety of circumstances. Subsequently, the planning team develops response protocols and procedures to support these efforts. Possible courses of action are typically developed using the following steps:

- **Depict the scenario.** Create a potential scenario based on the threats and hazards identified earlier in the planning process. For example, an earthquake occurs during the congregation's gathering which might include childcare or school activities. The facility may also be offered or rented for other activities, bringing many individuals to the site.

- **Determine the amount of time available to respond.** This will vary based on the type of threat or hazard and the particular scenario. For example, in the case of a hurricane, the house of worship might have days or hours to respond before the storm makes landfall, while the house of worship may have to respond in minutes to an active shooter.

---

[8] The term "annex" is used throughout this guide to refer to functional, threat/hazard-specific, or other supplements to the basic plan. Some plans may use the term "appendix" in the same fashion.

- **Identify decision points.** Decision points indicate the place in time, as threats or hazards unfold, when leaders anticipate making decisions about a course of action. Walking through each scenario in detail will help identify the relevant decision points for each scenario, such as whether to evacuate, shelter-in-place, or lockdown.

- **Develop courses of action.** Planners develop courses of action to achieve their goals and objectives by answering the following questions:

  - What is the action?

  - Who is responsible for the action?

  - When does the action take place?

  - Where does the action take place?

  - How long should the action take and how much time is actually available?

  - What has to happen before the action?

  - What happens after the action?

  - What resources and skills are needed to perform the action?

  - How will this action affect specific populations, such as children, the elderly, and individuals with disabilities and others with access and functional needs?

- **Select courses of action.** After developing courses of action, planners compare the costs and benefits of each proposed course of action against the goals and objectives. Based on this comparison, planners select the preferred course or courses of action to move forward in the planning process. Plans often include multiple courses of action for a given scenario to reflect the different ways it could unfold.

After selecting courses of action, the planning team should identify the resources necessary to accomplish each course of action without regard to resource availability. Once the planning team identifies all of the resource requirements, they begin matching available resources to the requirements. This step provides planners an opportunity to identify resource gaps or shortfalls that should be taken into account.

Step 4 Outcome

After completing Step 4, the planning team will have identified goals, objectives, and courses of action for before, during, and after threats and hazards, as well as functions. Goals, objectives, and courses of action for threats and hazards will be contained in the threat- and hazard-specific annexes in the plan. Goals, objectives, and courses of action for functions will be contained in the functional annexes of the plan.

Step 5: Plan Preparation, Review, and Approval

In Step 5, the planning team develops a draft of the EOP using the courses of action developed in Step 4. In addition, the team reviews the plan, obtains official approval, and shares the plan with community partners and stakeholders.

Format the Plan

An effective plan is presented in a way that makes it easy for users to find the information they need and that is compatible with local and state plans. This may include the use of plain language, providing pictures or visual cues for key action steps. This guide presents a traditional format that can be tailored to meet individual house of worship needs. This format has three major sections: the basic plan; functional annexes; and threat- and hazard-specific annexes.

The basic plan provides an overview of the house of worship's approach to emergency operations. Although the basic plan guides the development of the more operationally oriented annexes, its primary audience consists of the house of worship, local emergency management officials, and the community (as appropriate). The elements listed in this section should meet the needs of this audience while providing a solid foundation for the development of supporting annexes.

The functional annexes detail the goals, objectives, and courses of action of functions (e.g., evacuation, lockdown, and recovery) that apply across multiple threats or hazards. Functional annexes discuss how the house of worship manages a function before, during, and after an incident.

The threat- and hazard-specific annexes specify the goals, objectives, and courses of action that a house of worship will follow to address a particular type of threat or hazard (e.g., hurricane, active shooter). Threat- and hazard-specific annexes, like the functional annexes, discuss how the house of worship manages a threat or hazard before, during, and after an incident.

The following functional format can be used for the functional annexes as well as for the threat- and hazard-specific annexes. Using the format below and the work the planning team did in Step 4, each function, threat, and hazard will have at least three goals, with one or more objectives for each goal and a course of action for each objective.

Sample Annex Format

- Title (Function, Threat, or Hazard)
- Goal(s)
- Objective(s)
- Course(s) of Action (i.e., describe the courses of action developed in Step 4 in the sequence in which they will occur)

Figure 2 outlines the different components of each of these three sections. The "Plan Content" section of this guide discusses content for each of these components. The format presented in this guide can be used for both the basic plan and annexes. Each function, threat, or hazard will have at least three goals, with one or more objectives for each goal, and a course of action for each of the objectives. Each annex should specify the title of the annex and list the goals, objectives, and courses of action (in the sequence in which they would occur).

Basic Plan

1. Introductory Material
    1.1. Promulgation Document/Signatures
    1.2. Approval and Implementation
    1.3. Record and Changes
    1.4. Record of Distribution
    1.5. Table of Contents
2. Purpose and Situation Overview
    2.1. Purpose
    2.2. Situation Overview
3. Concept of Operations
4. Organization and Assignment of Responsibilities
5. Direction, Control, and Coordination
6. Information Collection, Analysis, and Dissemination
7. Training and Exercises
8. Administration, Finance, and Logistics
9. Plan Development and Maintenance
10. Authorities and References

Functional Annexes

(Note: This is not a complete list; however, it is recommended that all plans include these functional annexes.)

1. Evacuation
2. Lockdown
3. Shelter-in-Place
4. Recovery
5. Security

Hazard-, Threat-, or Incident-Specific Annexes

(NOTE: This is not a complete list. Each house of worship's annexes will vary based on their threat and hazard identification and risk assessment.)

1. Severe Storm
2. Earthquake
3. Tornado
4. Fire
5. Hazardous Materials Incident
6. Active Shooter

Figure 2: Sample EOP Format

Write the Plan

As the planning team works through successive drafts of the plan, the members add necessary tables, charts, and other supporting graphics. The planning team prepares and circulates a draft plan to obtain the comments of stakeholders that have responsibilities for implementing the plan. Successful plans are written following these simple rules:

- Use clear and simple writing in plain language. Summarize important information with checklists and visual aids, such as maps and flowcharts.

- Avoid using jargon and minimize the use of abbreviations.

- Use short sentences and the active voice. Qualifiers and vague wording only add to confusion.

- Use a logical, consistent structure that makes it easy for readers to understand the rationale for the sequence of information and to find the information they need.

- Provide enough detail to convey an easily understood plan that is actionable. Organize the contents in a way that helps users quickly identify solutions and options. Plans should provide guidance for carrying out common courses of action, through the functional- and threat and hazard-specific annexes, but "stay out of the weeds."

- Develop accessible tools and documents. Use appropriate auxiliary aids and services necessary for effective communication, such as accessible Web sites; digital text that can be converted to audio or Braille; the use of text equivalents for images; and captioning of any audio and audio description of any video content.

Review the Plan

Planners should check the written plan for compliance with applicable laws and for its usefulness in practice. Commonly used criteria can help determine the effectiveness and efficiency of the plan. The following measures can help determine if a plan is high quality.

- A plan is **adequate** if the plan identifies and addresses critical courses of action effectively; the plan can accomplish the assigned function; and the plan's assumptions are valid and reasonable.

- A plan is **feasible** if the house of worship can accomplish the assigned critical courses of action by using available resources within the time contemplated by the plan.

- A plan is **acceptable** if it meets the requirements driven by a threat or hazard, meets cost and time limitations, and is consistent with the law.

- A plan is **complete** if it:

  - Incorporates all courses of action to be accomplished for all selected threats and hazards and identified functions

  - Integrates the needs of the whole house of worship population

  - Provides a complete picture of what should happen, when, and at whose direction

  - Makes time estimates for achieving objectives, with safety remaining as the utmost priority

  - Identifies success criteria and a desired end-state

  - Is developed with the planning principles described in this guide.

- The plan should **comply** with applicable local and state requirements, because these provide a baseline that facilitates both planning and execution.

Additionally, when reviewing the plan, the planning team does not have to provide all of the resources needed to execute a course of action or meet a requirement established during the planning effort. However, the plan should explain where or how the house of worship would obtain the resources to support those requirements.

Approve and Share the Plan

After finalizing the plan, the planning team should present the plan to the appropriate leadership and obtain official approval of the plan. Once approval is granted, the planning team should share the plan with local emergency management officials, community partners that have a role in the plan, and organizations that may use the building(s). The planning team should maintain a record of the people and organizations that receive a copy of the plan.

Step 5 Outcome

After completing Step 5, the planning team will have a final EOP for the house of worship.

Step 6: Plan Implementation and Maintenance

Train Stakeholders on the Plan and Their Roles

Everyone involved in the plan needs to know their roles and responsibilities before, during, and after an incident. Key training components include:

- **Hold a meeting.** At least once a year, hold a meeting to educate all parties on the plan. Go through the plan in order to familiarize these stakeholders with it.

- **Visit evacuation sites.** Show involved parties not only where evacuation sites are located, but also where specific areas, such as reunification areas, media areas, and triage areas will be located.

- **Give stakeholders appropriate and relevant literature on the plan, policies, and procedures.** It may also be helpful to provide them with quick reference guides that remind them of key courses of action.

- **Post key information throughout the building.** It is important that congregants are familiar with and have easy access to information such as evacuation routes and shelter-in-place procedures and locations. Ensure information concerning evacuation routes and shelter-in-place procedures and locations is communicated effectively to congregants with disabilities or others with access and functional needs.

- **Familiarize congregants with the plan and community partners.** Bringing law enforcement, fire, and EMS personnel and community partners that have a role in the plan, as well as other organizations that use the building(s), into the house of worship to talk about the plan will make congregants and others more comfortable working with these partners. This may include community partners who are congregation members.

- **Train stakeholders on the skills necessary to fulfill their roles.** Persons will be assigned specific roles in the plan that will require special skills, such as first aid, how to use ICS, and the provision of personal assistance services for children, the elderly, and individuals with disabilities and others with access and functional needs.

Exercise the Plan

The more a plan is practiced and stakeholders are trained on the plan, the more effectively they will be able to act before, during, and after an incident to lessen the impact on life and property. Exercises provide opportunities to practice with local emergency management officials and community partners, as well as to identify gaps and weaknesses in the plan. The exercises below require increasing amounts of planning, time, and resources. Ideally, houses of worship will create an exercise program, building from a tabletop up to a more advanced exercise, like a functional exercise.[9]

- **Tabletop exercises** are small group discussions that walk through a scenario and the courses of action a house of worship will need to take before, during, and after an incident. This

---

[9] For additional information on conducting exercises, please see the Homeland Security Exercise and Evaluation Program Web site at http://hseep.dhs.gov.

activity helps assess the plan and resources and facilitates an understanding of emergency management and planning concepts.

- During **drills**, local emergency management officials, community partners, and relevant house of worship personnel use the actual house of worship grounds and buildings to practice responding to a scenario.

- **Functional exercises** are similar to drills, but involve multiple partners. Participants react to realistic simulated events (e.g., a bomb threat, or an intruder with a gun), and implement the plan and procedures using ICS.

- **Full-scale exercises** are the most time-consuming activity in the exercise continuum and are multiagency, multi-jurisdiction efforts in which resources are deployed. This type of exercise tests collaboration among the agencies and participants, public information systems, communications systems, and equipment. An emergency operations center is established (usually by the local emergency management agency) and ICS is activated.

Before making a decision about how many and which types of exercises to implement, a house of worship should consider the costs and benefits. Houses of worship should also consider having representative(s) participate in larger community exercises to ensure that their efforts are synchronized with the whole community's efforts.

It is up to the planning team to decide how often exercises should be conducted. While frequent exercise is important, it is imperative that exercises are high quality. To conduct an exercise effectively:

- Include local emergency management officials and community partners

- Communicate information in advance to avoid confusion and concern

- Exercise under different and non-ideal conditions (e.g., time of day, weather)

- Be consistent with common emergency management terminology

- Debrief and develop an after-action report that evaluates results; identifies gaps or shortfalls; and documents lessons learned

- Discuss how the plan and procedures will be modified, if needed, and specify who has the responsibility for modifying the plan.

Review, Revise, and Maintain the Plan

Planning is a continuous process that does not stop when the plan is published. Plans should evolve as lessons are learned; new information and insights are obtained; new threats or hazards emerge; and priorities are updated. Reviews should be a recurring activity. Planning teams should establish a process for reviewing and revising the plan. Many organizations review their plans on an annual basis. In no case should any part of the plan go for more than two years without being reviewed and revised.

Some organizations have found it useful to review and revise portions instead of reviewing the entire plan at once. Certain events will also provide new information that will be used to inform the plan. Houses of worship should consider reviewing and updating their plan after the following events:

- Actual emergencies

- Changes in policy, personnel, organizational structures, processes, facilities, equipment, or membership size

- Formal updates of planning guidance or standards

- Formal exercises

- Threats or hazards change or new threats or hazards emerge

- Changes in the house of worship's demographics (e.g., changing language needs) or site assessment.

The planning team should ensure that all local emergency management officials and community partners have the most current version of the house of worship's plan.

Plan Content

Step 5 of the planning process in this guide introduced a format with three sections for houses of worship to follow in developing an EOP. This section provides greater detail about what each of the three sections should include and provides some key considerations in developing the content.

Basic Plan

The basic plan provides an overview of the house of worship's approach to operations before, during, and after an incident. This section addresses the overarching activities the house of worship undertakes regardless of the function, threat, or hazard. The content in this section provides a solid foundation for the house of worship's operations. The information in this section should not duplicate information contained in other sections of the plan. Almost all of the information contained in the basic plan should be able to come from the planning team. If the planning team finds that it has to go outside the planning team for a significant amount of information, it may be an indication that the planning team membership needs to be expanded.

Introductory Material

Introductory material can enhance accountability with local emergency management officials and community partners and make a plan easier to use. Typical introductory material includes:

- **Cover Page.** The cover page has the title of the plan. It should include a date and identify the house of worship covered by the plan.

- **Promulgation Document/Signature Page.** This document/page is a signed statement formally recognizing and adopting the plan as the house of worship's plan. It gives both the authority and the responsibility to house of worship leadership to perform their tasks before, during, or after an incident, and therefore should be signed by the house of worship's senior leadership.

- **Approval and Implementation Page.** The approval and implementation page introduces the plan, outlines its applicability, and indicates that it supersedes all previous plans. It should include a delegation of authority for specific modifications that can be made to the plan and by whom they can be made without the signature of leadership. It should also include a date and should be signed by the house of worship's senior leadership.

- **Record of Changes.** Each update or change to the plan should be tracked. The record of changes, usually in table format, contains, at a minimum, a change number, the date of the change, the name of the person who made the change, and a summary of the change.

- **Record of Distribution.** The record of distribution, usually in table format, indicates the title and the name of the person receiving the plan, the organization to which the recipient belongs, the date of delivery, and the number of copies delivered. Other relevant information could be considered. The record of distribution can be used to prove that tasked individuals and organizations have acknowledged their receipt, review, and/or acceptance of the plan.

- **Table of Contents.** The table of contents is a logically ordered and clearly identified layout of the major sections and subsections of the plan that will make finding information within the plan easier.

Purpose and Situation Overview

This section includes the following components:

- **Purpose.** The purpose sets the foundation for the rest of the plan. The basic plan's purpose is a general statement of what the plan is meant to do. The statement should be supported by a brief synopsis of the basic plan and annexes.

- **Situation Overview.** The situation overview explains why the plan is necessary. The situation overview covers a general discussion of:

  - The threats and hazards that pose a risk to the house of worship and would result in a need to use this plan

  - Dependencies on parties outside the house of worship for critical resources

Concept of Operations

This section explains in broad terms the decision maker's intent with regard to an operation. This section provides an overall impression of how the house of worship will protect its occupants and should:

- Identify those with authority to activate the plan

- Describe the process by which the house of worship coordinates with all appropriate agencies within the jurisdiction

- Describe how plans take into account the architectural, programmatic, and communication needs of children, the elderly, and individuals with disabilities and others with access and functional needs (including their service animals)

- Identify other response/support agency plans that directly support the implementation of the plan (e.g., city or county EOP)

- Explain that the primary purpose of actions taken before an incident is to prevent, protect from, and mitigate the impact on life or property

- Explain that the primary purpose of actions taken during an incident is to respond to the incident and minimize its impact on life or property

- Explain that the primary purpose of actions taken after an incident is to recover from its impact on life or property

Organization and Assignment of Responsibilities

This section provides an overview of the broad roles and responsibilities of house of worship leadership and staff; local emergency management officials; and community partners and an overview of organizational functions during all incidents. This section should:

- Describe the roles and responsibilities of each individual/organization that apply during an incident (response), including, but not limited to, house of worship leadership, staff, lay leadership, congregants, and local departments and agencies (e.g., fire, law enforcement, EMS, emergency management) [10]

- Describe informal and formal agreements in place for the quick activation and sharing of resources during an incident (e.g., evacuation locations to a nearby business' parking lot). Agreements may be between the house of worship and response organizations (e.g., fire, law enforcement, EMS), other houses of worship, organizations, and businesses.

Direction, Control, and Coordination

This section describes the framework for all direction, control, and coordination activities. This section should:

- Describe the chain of command used by the house of worship

- Describe the relationship between the house of worship's plan and the broader community's emergency management system

- Describe who has control of equipment, resources, and supplies needed to support the plan.

Information Collection, Analysis, and Dissemination

This section addresses the role of information in the successful implementation of the activities that occur before, during, and after an incident. This section should:

- Identify the type of information that will be helpful in the successful implementation of the activities that occur before, during, and after an emergency, such as:

  - Before and during: weather reports, law enforcement alerts, National Oceanic and Atmospheric Administration radio alerts, and crime reports

  - After: Web sites and hotlines for mental health agencies, emergency management agencies, and relief agencies assisting in all aspects of recovery.

- Provide answers to the following questions for each of the identified types of information:

  - What is the source of the information?

  - Who analyzes and uses the information?

---

[10] If the planning team considers the information critical to the successful implementation of the plan, it may identify roles and responsibilities of one or more individuals/organizations before and after an incident in addition to during the incident.

- How is the information collected and shared?
- What is the format for providing the information to those who will use it?
- When should the information be collected and shared?

Training and Exercises

This section describes the critical training and exercise activities the house of worship will use in support of the plan. This includes the core training objectives and frequency to ensure that stakeholders understand roles, responsibilities, and expectations. This section also establishes the expected frequency of exercises to be conducted by the house of worship. Content may be influenced based on similar requirements at the local level (e.g., the local emergency management agency's exercise schedule). Exercises may range from basic fire and shelter-in-place drills to full-scale community-wide drills.

Administration, Finance, and Logistics

This section covers general support requirements and the availability of services and support for all types of incidents, as well as general policies for managing resources. It should identify and reference policies and procedures that exist outside of the plan. This section should:

- Identify administrative controls and requirements that will be used to provide resource and expenditure accountability
- Briefly describe how the house of worship will maintain accurate logs of key activities
- Briefly describe how vital records will be preserved
- Identify sources for replacement of assets
- Identify general policies for keeping financial records; tracking resource needs; tracking the source and use of resources; acquiring ownership of resources; and compensating the owners of private property used by the house of worship.

Plan Development and Maintenance

This section discusses the overall approach to planning and the assignment of plan development and maintenance responsibilities. This section should:

- Describe the planning process, participants in that process, and how development and revision of different sections of the plan (i.e., basic plan, annexes) are coordinated prior to an incident
- Assign responsibility for the overall planning and coordination to a specific position or person
- Provide for a regular cycle of training, evaluating, reviewing, and updating of the plan.

Authorities and References

This section provides the legal basis for emergency operations and includes:

- Lists of laws, statutes, ordinances, executive orders, regulations, and formal agreements relevant to emergencies in the community

- Provisions for the succession of decisionmaking authority and operational control to ensure that critical emergency functions can be performed in the absence of the house of worship's senior leadership.

Functional Annexes

Functional annexes focus on critical operational functions and the courses of action developed to carry them out. This section describes functional annexes that the house of worship should develop as part of the plan. As the planning team assesses the house of worship's needs, it may need to prepare additional or different annexes. Also included in this section are issues the planning team should consider as it develops goals, objectives, and courses of action for these functions. These are some of the most important issues, but this is not meant to be an exhaustive list.

Functions may occur consecutively or concurrently, depending on the incident. While functions build upon one another and overlap, it is not necessary to repeat a course of action in one functional annex if it appears in a second functional annex. For example, though an evacuation may lead to reunification, it not necessary to list a course of action for reunification within the evacuation annex.

Evacuation Annex

This annex focuses on the courses of action that the house of worship will execute to evacuate buildings and grounds. The planning team should consider the following when developing their goals, objectives, and courses of action:

- How to safely move persons to designated assembly areas from buildings and outside areas

- How to evacuate when the primary route evacuation route is unusable

- How to evacuate children who are not with a parent or guardian

- How to evacuate senior citizens and individuals with disabilities (along with service animals and assistive devices) and others with access and functional needs, including language, transportation, and medical needs.

Lockdown Annex

This annex focuses on the courses of action the house of worship will execute to secure buildings and grounds during incidents that pose an immediate threat of violence in or around the house of worship. The primary objective of a lockdown is to ensure all persons are secured quickly in the rooms away from immediate danger. The planning team should consider the following when developing their goals, objectives, and courses of action:

- How to lock all exterior doors and when it may or may not be safe to do so

- How particular building characteristics (e.g., windows, doors) affect possible lockdown courses of action

- What to do when a threat materializes inside the house of worship

- When to use the different variations of a lockdown (e.g., when outside activities are curtailed, doors are locked, and visitors closely monitored but all other activities continue as normal).

Shelter-in-Place Annex

A shelter-in-place annex focuses on courses of action when persons are required to remain indoors, perhaps for an extended period, because it is safer inside the building or a room than outside. Depending on the threat or hazard, persons may be required to move to rooms that can be sealed (such as in the event of a chemical or biological hazard) or without windows, or to a weather shelter (such as in the event of a tornado). The planning team should consider the following when developing their goals, objectives, and courses of action:

- What supplies will be needed to seal the room and to provide for personal needs (e.g., water)

- How shelter-in-place can affect individuals with disabilities and others with access and functional needs, such as persons who require the regular administration of medication, durable medical equipment, and personal assistant services

- How to move persons when the primary route is unusable

- How to locate and move children who are not with a parent or guardian

- Consider the need for and integration of "safe rooms" for protection against extreme wind hazards (such as a tornado or hurricane) in order to provide immediate life-safety protection when evacuation is not an option.

Recovery Annex

This annex describes how the house of worship will recover from an emergency. The four fundamental kinds of recovery are services recovery; physical recovery; fiscal recovery; and psychological and emotional recovery. The planning team should consider the following when developing their goals, objectives, and courses of action:

- Services Recovery
  - When and who has the authority to close and reopen the house of worship
  - What temporary space(s) may be used if buildings cannot be immediately reopened
  - How alternate services will be provided in the event that congregation members cannot physically reconvene.

- Physical Recovery
  - How assets are documented, including physically accessible facilities, in case of damage
  - Which personnel have expert knowledge of the assets and how and where they will access records to verify current assets after an emergency
  - How the house of worship will work with utility and insurance companies before an emergency to support a quicker recovery.

- Fiscal Recovery
  - How will staff receive timely and factual information regarding returning to work
  - What sources the house of worship may access for emergency relief funding.

- Psychological and Emotional Recovery:
  - Who will serve as the leader

- Where will counseling and psychological first aid be provided

- How members will create a calm and supportive environment for the congregation, share basic information about the incident, provide psychological first aid (if trained), and identify members and staff who may need immediate crisis counseling

- Who will provide trained counselors

- How to address immediate-, short-, and long-term counseling needs of staff members and families

- How to handle commemorations, memorial activities, or permanent markers and/or memorial structures (if any will be allowed); including concerns such as when a commemoration site will be closed, what will be done with notes/tributes, and how the congregation will be informed in advance

- How memorial activities will strike a balance among honoring the loss; resuming routines and schedules; and maintaining hope for the future.

Security Annex

This annex focuses on the courses of action that the house of worship will implement on a routine, ongoing basis to secure the house of worship from criminal threats, including efforts done in conjunction with law enforcement.

Threat- and Hazard-Specific Annexes

The threat- and hazard-specific annexes describe the courses of action unique to particular threats and hazards. Courses of action already outlined in a functional annex need not be repeated in a threat- or hazard-specific annex. A house of worship will develop these based on the prioritized list of threats and hazards determined during the planning process. As planning teams develop courses of action for threats and hazards, they should consider the local, state, and Federal regulations or mandates that often apply to specific hazard. Table 2 provides example threats and hazards for which a house of worship may need to plan.

Table 2: Example Threats and Hazards

Threat/Hazard Type	Examples
Natural Hazards	<ul><li>Earthquakes</li><li>Tornadoes</li><li>Lightning</li><li>Severe wind</li><li>Hurricanes</li><li>Floods</li><li>Wildfires</li><li>Extreme temperatures</li><li>Landslides or mudslides</li><li>Tsunamis</li><li>Volcanic eruptions</li><li>Winter precipitation</li></ul>

Threat/Hazard Type	Examples
Technological Hazards	• Explosions or accidental releases from industrial plants • Hazardous materials releases from major highways or railroads • Radiological releases from nuclear power stations • Dam failure • Power failure • Water failure
Adversarial and Human-caused Threats	• Arson • Active shooters • Criminal or gang violence • Violence related to domestic disputes • Bomb • Cyber attacks

If there is a functional annex that applies to one of the threat- or hazard-specific annexes, the threat- or hazard-specific annex will include it by reference.

For example if a *during* course of action for a fire hazard involves evacuation and there is an evacuation functional annex, the fire annex would state "see evacuation annex" in the fire annex's *during* course of action section rather than repeat the evacuation courses of action in the fire annex.

A Closer Look: Active Shooter Situations

Police officers, firefighters, and EMS (i.e., first responders) who come to a house of worship because of a 911 call involving gunfire face a daunting task. Though the objective—protect congregants—remains the same, the threat of an active shooter incident is different from responding to a natural disaster or other emergencies.

Active shooter situations are defined as those where an individual is "actively engaged in killing or attempting to kill people in a confined and populated area."[11] Unfortunately, houses of worship are not immune from this tragedy. For example, in 2012, six people were killed and four injured in a shooting at a Sikh temple in Oak Creek, Wisconsin, and in 2008, two people were killed and seven wounded at a Unitarian Church in Knoxville, Tennessee.

The better first responders and those working and visiting a house of worship are able to discern these threats and react swiftly, the more lives can be saved. This is particularly true in an active shooter situation, where law enforcement responds to a 911 call of shots fired. Many innocent lives are at risk in a concentrated area. Working with emergency management officials and community partners, houses of worship can develop a plan to better prepare their staff and congregants in prevention, reaction, and response to an active shooter incident.

---

[11] DHS. 2008. *Active Shooter: How to Respond.* Washington, DC: DHS. http://www.dhs.gov/xlibrary/assets/active_shooter_booklet.pdf. Other gun-related incidents that may occur in a house of worship are not defined as active shooter incidents because they do not meet this definition. Instead, they may involve a single shot fired, accidental discharge of a weapon, or incidents that are not ongoing.

Active shooter situations are unpredictable and evolve quickly. Because of this, individuals must be prepared to deal with an active shooter situation before law enforcement arrives on the scene.

Preparing for an Active Shooter Incident

Planning

As with any threat or hazard that is included in a house of worship's EOP, the planning team will establish goals, objectives, and courses of action for an active shooter annex. These plans will be affected by the assessments conducted at the outset of the planning process and updated as ongoing assessments occur. As courses of action are developed, the planning team should consider a number of issues, including, but not limited to:

- How to evacuate or lockdown personnel and visitors. Personnel involved in such planning should pay attention to disability-related accessibility concerns when advising on shelter sites and evacuation routes

- How to evacuate when the primary evacuation routes are unusable

- How to select effective shelter-in-place locations (optimal locations have thick walls, solid doors with locks, minimal interior windows, first aid-emergency kits, communication devices and duress alarms)

- How those present in buildings and on the ground will be notified that there is an active shooter incident underway. This could be done using familiar terms, sounds, lights, and electronic communications, such as text messages or emails. Include in the courses of action how to communicate with those who have language barriers or need other accommodations, such as visual signals to communicate with hearing-impaired individuals. Planners should make sure this protocol is readily available and understood by those who may be responsible for sending out or broadcasting an announcement. Rapid notification of a threat can save lives by keeping people out of harm's way.

- How everyone will know when buildings and grounds are safe.

The planning team may want to include functions in the active shooter annex that are also addressed in other functional annexes. For example, evacuation will be different during an active shooter situation than it would be for a fire.

Additional considerations are included in the "Responding to an Active Shooter Incident" and "After an Active Shooter Incident" sections below.

Sharing Information with First Responders

The planning process is not complete until the house of worship's EOP is shared with first responders. The planning process should include preparing and making available to first responders an up-to-date and well-documented site assessment as well as any other information that would assist them. These materials should include building schematics and photos of the buildings, both inside and out, and include information about door and window locations, as well as locks and access controls. Emergency responders should also have advance information on where individuals with disabilities are likely to be sheltering or escaping, generally in physically accessible locations or along accessible routes. Building strong partnerships with law enforcement, fire, and EMS includes ensuring they also know the location of available public address systems, two-way communications systems, security cameras, and alarm controls. Equally important is information on access to utility controls, medical supplies, and fire extinguishers.

Providing detailed information to first responders allows them to rapidly move through buildings and the grounds during an emergency; to ensure areas are safe; and to tend to those in need. It is critically important to share this information with law enforcement and other first responders before an emergency occurs so that they have immediate access to the information. Law enforcement agencies have secure Web sites where these items already are stored for many schools, business, public venues, and other locations. All of these can be provided to first responders and viewed in drills, exercises, and walkthroughs.

Technology and tools with the same information (e.g., a portable USB drive that is compatible with computers used by first responders) should be maintained in secured locations in the building where designated staff for the house of worship can immediately provide it to responding officials, or where first responders can directly access it. The locations of these materials should be known by and accessible to a number of individuals to ensure ready access in an emergency. Every house of worship should have more than one individual charged with meeting first responders to provide them with the site assessment, the EOP, and any other details about facility safety or concerns.[12]

Exercises

Evacuation drills for fires and protective measures for tornadoes may be part of routine activities for a house of worship, but far fewer facilities practice for active shooter situations. To be prepared for an active shooter incident, houses of worship should train their staff and congregation, as appropriate, in what to expect and how to react.

Good planning includes conducting drills that involve first responders. Exercises with these valuable partners are one of the most effective and efficient ways to ensure that everyone knows not only their role, but also the role of others at the scene. These exercises should include walks through buildings to allow law enforcement to provide input on shelter sites as well as familiarize first responders with the location.

> Each person carries a responsibility that is three-fold:
> 1. Learn the signs of a potentially volatile situation and ways to prevent an incident.
> 2. Learn the best steps for survival when faced with an active shooter situation.
> 3. Be prepared to work with law enforcement during the response.

Preventing an Active Shooter Incident

Warning Signs

No profile exists for an active shooter; however, research indicates there may be signs or indicators. Leaders and staff in houses of worship counsel congregants on a daily basis as part of

---

[12] For additional information, please see http://www.ready.gov.

their work. Law enforcement can assist in knowing the signs of a potentially volatile situation and help houses of worship proactively seek ways to prevent an incident from escalating.

By highlighting common pre-attack behaviors displayed by past offenders, Federal researchers have sought to enhance the detection and prevention of tragic attacks of violence, including active shooting incidents. Several agencies within the Federal Government continue to explore incidents of targeted violence in the effort to identify these potential "warning signs." In 2002, the Federal Bureau of Investigation (FBI) published a monograph on workplace violence, including problematic behaviors of concern that may telegraph violent ideations and plans.[13]

Specialized units in the Federal Government (such as the FBI's Behavioral Analysis Unit) continue to support behaviorally-based operational assessments of persons of concern in a variety of settings (e.g. schools, workplaces, houses of worship) who appear to be on a trajectory toward a catastrophic violent act. A review of current research, threat assessment literature, and active shooting incidents, combined with the extensive case experience of the Behavioral Analysis Unit, suggest that there are observable pre-attack behaviors which, if recognized, could lead to the disruption of a planned attack.[14] While checklists of various "warning signs" are often of limited use in isolation, there are some behavioral indicators that should prompt further exploration and attention from law enforcement and/or house of worship officials. These behaviors often include:

- Development of a personal grievance

- Contextually inappropriate and recent acquisitions of multiple weapons

- Contextually inappropriate and recent escalation in target practice and weapons training

- Contextually inappropriate and recent interest in explosives

- Contextually inappropriate and intense interest or fascination with previous shootings or mass attacks

- Many offenders experienced a significant real or perceived personal loss in the weeks and/or months leading up to the attack, such as a death, breakup, divorce, or loss of a job

- Few offenders had previous arrests for violent crimes.

No research has been conducted on individuals solely engaged in active shooting incidents at houses of worship; however, the behaviors listed above may be useful in identifying some of the behaviors of individuals of potential concern.[15]

---

[13] FBI. 2002. *Workplace Violence: Issues in Response.* Quantico, VA: FBI. http://www.fbi.gov/stats-services/publications/workplace-violence

[14] See *Contemporary Threat Management: A Practical Guide for Identifying, Assessing, and Managing Individuals of Violent Intent* (Specialized Training Services, 2003); *The Handbook for Campus Threat Assessment and Management Teams* (Applied Risk Management, 2008); *Threat Assessment: An Approach to Prevent Targeted Violence* (U.S. Department of Justice, 1995); and *Rethinking Risk Assessment: The MacArthur Study of Mental Disorder and Violence* (Oxford University Press, 2001).

[15] For information on warning signs of violence at schools, see *The Final Report and Findings of the Safe School Initiative: Implications for the Prevention of School Attacks in the United States* (U.S. Secret Service and U.S. Department of Education, 2004) and *Threat Assessment in Schools: A Guide to Managing Threatening Situations and to Creating Safe School Climates* (U.S. Secret Service and U.S. Department of Education, 2002). Additionally, in 2007 the U.S. Secret Service, FBI, and U.S. Department of Education initiated an examination of attempted and

Threat Assessment Teams

As described in the previous section, research shows that perpetrators of targeted acts of violence engage in both covert and overt behaviors preceding their attacks. They consider, plan, prepare, share, and, in some cases, move on to action. A useful tool to identify, evaluate, and address these troubling signs is the creation of a multidisciplinary Threat Assessment Team (TAT) for the house of worship.[16] The TAT serves as a central convening body, so that warning signs observed by multiple people are not considered isolated incidents, slipping through the cracks, when they actually may represent escalating behavior that is a serious concern. TATs should keep in mind, however, the importance of relying on facts (including observed behavior) and avoid unfair labeling or stereotyping of individuals to remain in compliance with civil rights laws, when applicable.

Although not as common in private industry or in religious establishments, TATs are increasingly common in college and university settings, pushed to the forefront of concern following the 2007 shooting at Virginia Polytechnic Institute and State University, Blacksburg, Virginia, where 32 individuals were killed. In some cases, state funding mandates that institutions of higher learning create TATs.[17] Houses of worship may also want to create TATs. The Departments offer the following recommendations for the creation and operation of TATs, although they fully recognize that houses of worship may differ in their approaches to certain issues.

For the purposes of consistency and efficiency, a TAT should be developed and implemented in coordination with other policy and practices for the organization. A TAT with diverse representation often will operate more efficiently and effectively. TAT members may include the leaders or administrators of the house of worship, counselors, staff, congregants, and medical and mental health professionals, who may be drawn from the congregation.

TATs review troubling or threatening behavior of persons brought to the attention of the TAT. TATs contemplate a holistic assessment and management strategy that considers the many aspects of the person's life. More than focusing on warning signs or threats alone, a TAT assessment involves a unique overall analysis of changing and relevant behaviors. The TAT takes into consideration, as appropriate, information about behaviors; communications; any threats made; security concerns; family issues; or relationship problems that might involve a troubled individual. The TAT may also identify any potential victims with whom the individual may interact. Once the TAT identifies an individual that may pose a threat, the team will identify a course of action for addressing the situation. The appropriate course of action, whether law

---

committed homicidal acts of violence on American college campuses from 1900 to 2008, *Campus Attacks: Targeted Violence Affecting Institutions of Higher Education* (U.S. Secret Service, et al., 2010, http://www2.ed.gov/admins/lead/safety/campus-attacks.pdf). A second phase of the project focuses exclusively on grievance-based attacks that occurred from 1985 to 2010.

[16] Albrecht, Steve. 2010. "Threat Assessment Teams: Workplace and School Violence Prevention." *FBI Law Enforcement Bulletin (February 2010)*. http://www.fbi.gov/stats-services/publications/law-enforcement-bulletin/february-2010/threat-assessment-teams

[17] For example, please see http://leg1.state.va.us/cgi-bin/legp504.exe?000+cod+23-9.2C10. Additional information can be found in *Recommended Practices for Virginia Colleges Threat Assessments* (Virginia Department of Criminal Justice Services, 2009, http://www.threatassessment.vt.edu/resources/tat_info/VArecommended_practices.pdf).

enforcement intervention, counseling, or other actions, will depend on the specifics of the situation.

The TAT may wish to seek assistance from law enforcement that can help assess reported threats or troubling behavior and tap available Federal resources (as part of the TAT process or separately). The FBI's behavioral experts in its National Center for the Analysis of Violent Crimes (NCAVC) at Quantico, Virginia are available on a 24 hours per day, seven days per week basis to join in any threat assessment analysis and develop threat mitigation strategies for persons of concern. Law enforcement working with a TAT from a house of worship should contact the local FBI office for this behavioral analysis assistance.

Each FBI field office has a NCAVC representative available to work with the house of worship TAT and coordinate access to the FBI's Behavioral Analysis Unit, if the congregation wishes. They focus not on how to respond tactically to an active shooter situation, but rather on how to prevent one. Early intervention can prevent a situation from escalating by identifying, assessing, and managing the threat.

Houses of worship should also work with local law enforcement to gain an understanding of the threats from outside the house of worship community that may affect the facility, so that, in partnership, appropriate security measures can be established.

Generally, active shooter situations are not motivated by other criminal-related concerns such as monetary gain or gang affiliation. Often, violence may be prevented by identifying, assessing, and managing potential threats. Recognizing these pre-attack warning signs and indicators might help disrupt a potentially tragic event.

Responding to an Active Shooter Incident

The house of worship's EOP should include courses of action that will describe how congregants and staff can most effectively respond to an active shooter situation to minimize the loss of life, and teach and train on these practices.

Law enforcement officers may not be present when a shooting begins. Providing information on how congregants and staff can respond to the incident can help prevent and reduce the loss of life.

No single response fits all active shooter situations; however, making sure each individual knows his or her options for response and can react decisively will save valuable time. Depicting scenarios and considering response options in advance will assist individuals and groups in quickly selecting their best course of action.

Understandably, this is a sensitive topic. There is no single answer for what to do, but a survival mindset can increase the odds of surviving. As appropriate for the house of worship's congregation, it may be valuable to schedule a time for an open conversation regarding this topic. Though some congregants or staff may find the conversation uncomfortable, they may also find it reassuring to know that as a whole their house of worship is thinking about how best to deal with this situation.

During an active shooter situation, the natural human reaction, even for those who are highly trained, is to be startled; feel fear and anxiety; and even experience initial disbelief and denial. Noise from alarms, gunfire, explosions, and people shouting and screaming should be expected. Training provides the means to regain composure, recall at least some of what has been learned, and commit to action. There are three basic response options: run, hide, or fight. Individuals can run away from the shooter; seek a secure place where they can hide and/or deny the shooter access; or incapacitate the shooter in order to survive and protect others from harm.

As the situation develops, it is possible that congregants and staff will need to use more than one option. During an active shooter situation, these individuals will rarely have all of the information they need to make a fully informed decision about which option is best. While they should follow the plan and any instructions given during an incident, they will often have to rely on their own judgment to decide which option will best protect lives.[18]

Respond Immediately

It is common for people confronted with a threat to first deny the possible danger rather than respond. An investigation by the National Institute of Standards and Technology (2005) into the collapse of the World Trade Center towers on September 11, 2001 found that people close to the affected floors waited longer to start evacuating than those on unaffected floors.[19] Similarly, during the Virginia Tech shooting, individuals on campus responded to the shooting with varying degrees of urgency.[20] These studies support this delayed response or denial. For example, some people report hearing firecrackers, when in fact they heard gunfire. Train congregants and staff to skip denial and to respond immediately.

For example, train congregants to recognize the sounds of danger, act, and forcefully communicate the danger and necessary action (e.g., "Gun! Get out!"). In addition, those closest to a communications system should communicate the danger and necessary action. Repetition in training and preparedness shortens the time it takes to orient, observe, and act. Upon recognizing the danger, as soon as it is safe to do so staff or others should alert responders by contacting 911 with as clear and accurate information as possible.

Run

If it is safe to do so, the first course of action that should be taken is to run out of the building and far away until in a safe location. Congregants and staff should be trained to:

- Leave personal belongings behind
- Visualize possible escape routes, including physically accessible routes for individuals with disabilities
- Avoid escalators and elevators

---

[18] As part of its preparedness mission, *Ready Houston* produces videos, handouts, and trainings to promote preparedness among residents of the Houston, Texas region. These videos are not recommended for viewing by minors. All of these items are available free-of-charge and many are available at http://wwww.readyhoustontx.gov/videos.html.

[19] Occupants of both towers delayed initiating their evacuation after WTC 1 was hit. In WTC 1, the median time to initiate evacuation was three minutes for occupants from the ground floor to floor 76, and five minutes for occupants near the impact region (floors 77 to 91). Averill, Jason D., et al. 2005. *Federal Building and Fire Safety Investigation of the World Trade Center Disaster: Occupant Behavior, Egress, and Emergency Communications.* Washington, DC: National Institute of Standards and Technology. http://www.mingerfoundation.org/downloads/mobility/nist%20world%20trade%20center.pdf

[20] Virginia Tech Review Panel. 2007. *Mass Shootings at Virginia Tech: Report of the Review Panel.* Richmond, VA: Virginia Tech Review Panel. http://www.governor.virginia.gov/tempContent/techPanelReport-docs/FullReport.pdf

- Take others with them, but do not stay behind because others will not go
- Call 911 when safe to do so
- Let a responsible adult know where they are.

Hide

If running is not a safe option, hide in as safe a place as possible. Congregants and staff should be trained to hide in a location where the walls might be thicker and have fewer windows. In addition:

- Lock the doors
- Barricade the doors with heavy furniture
- Close and lock windows and close blinds or cover windows
- Turn off lights
- Silence all electronic devices
- Remain silent
- If possible, use strategies to silently communicate with first responders; for example, in rooms with exterior windows, make signs to silently signal law enforcement and emergency responders to indicate the status of the room's occupants
- Hide along the wall closest to the exit but out of the view from the hallway (allowing for an ambush of the shooter and for possible escape if the shooter enters the room)
- Remain in place until given an all clear by identifiable law enforcement.

Fight

If neither running nor hiding is a safe option, as a last resort, when confronted by the shooter, adults in immediate danger should consider trying to disrupt or incapacitate the shooter by using aggressive force and items in their environment, such as fire extinguishers or chairs. In a study of 41 active shooter events that ended before law enforcement arrived, the potential victims stopped the attacker themselves in 16 instances. In 13 of those cases, they physically subdued the attacker.[21]

While talking to the congregation and staff about confronting a shooter may be daunting and upsetting for some, they should know that they might be able to successfully take action to save lives. How each individual chooses to respond if directly confronted by an active shooter is up to him or her. Each house of worship should determine, as part of its planning process, policies on the control and presence of weapons, as permitted by law.

---

[21] Blair, J. Pete and M. Hunter Martaindale. 2010. *United States Active Shooter Events from 2000 to 2010: Training and Equipment Implications*. San Marcos, TX: Texas State University. http://alerrt.org/files/research/ActiveShooterEvents.pdf

Interacting with First Responders

If a shooting occurs, congregants and staff should be trained to understand and expect that law enforcement's first priority must be to locate and stop the person or persons believed to be the shooter(s); all other actions are secondary. One comprehensive study found that in more than half of mass shooting incidents where a solo officer arrived on the scene (57 percent) shooting was still underway when the officer arrived. In 75 percent of those instances, that solo officer had to confront the perpetrator to end the threat. In those cases, the officer was shot one-third of the time.[22]

Congregants and staff should be trained to cooperate and not to interfere with first responders. They should display empty hands with open palms and anticipate that law enforcement may instruct everyone to place their hands on their heads or get on the ground.

After an Active Shooter Incident[23]

Once the scene is secured, first responders will work with house of worship staff and victims on a variety of matters. This will include transporting the injured, interviewing witnesses, and initiating the investigation.

The house of worship's EOP should identify trained personnel who will provide assistance to victims and their families. This should include establishing an incident response team (including community partners) that is trained to appropriately assess and triage an active shooter situation (as well as other emergencies), and provide emergency intervention services and victim assistance beginning immediately after the incident and throughout the recovery efforts. This team will integrate with local, state, and Federal resources when an emergency occurs.

Within an ongoing and/or evolving emergency, where the immediate reunification of loved ones is not possible, providing family members with timely, accurate, and relevant information is paramount. Having family members wait for long periods for information about their loved ones not only adds to their stress and frustration, but can also escalate the emotions of the entire group. When families are reunited, it is critical that there are child release processes in place where minors might be involved (e.g., childcare, religious classes) to assure that no child is released to an unauthorized person, even if that person well meaning.

Essential steps to help establish trust and provide family members with a sense of control can be accomplished by:

- Identifying a safe location separate from distractions and/or media and the general public, but close enough to allow family members to feel connected in proximity to their children/loved ones

- Scheduling periodic updates even if no additional information is available

- Being prepared to speak with family members about what to expect when reunified with their child/loved ones

---

[22] Ibid.

[23] Please see the "Functional Annexes" section of this guide for additional recovery annex considerations.

- Ensuring effective communication with those that have language barriers or need other accommodations, such as sign language interpreters for the hearing impaired.

When reunification is not possible because an individual is missing, injured, or killed, how and when this information is provided to families is critical. Before an emergency, the planning team should determine how, when, and by whom loved ones will be informed if their loved one is missing or has been injured or killed. Law enforcement typically takes the lead on death notifications, but all parties should understand their roles and responsibilities. This will ensure that families and loved ones receive accurate and timely information in a compassionate way.

While law enforcement and medical examiner procedures must be followed, families should receive accurate information as soon as possible. Having trained personnel to talk to loved ones about death and injury on hand or immediately available can ensure the notification is provided to family members with clarity and compassion. Counselors should be on hand to immediately assist family members.

The house of worship's EOP should include identified points of contact to work with and support family members (e.g., Federal victim assistance personnel, counselors, police officers). These points of contact should be connected to families as early in the process as possible, including while an individual is still missing but before any victims have been positively identified. After an incident, it is critical to confirm that each family is getting the support it needs, including long-term support.

The house of worship's EOP should consider printed and age-appropriate resources to help families recognize and seek help in regard to a variety of reactions that they or their loved ones can experience during and after an emergency. It is critical that families and loved ones are supported as they both grieve their loss and support their surviving family members.

The house of worship's EOP also should explicitly address how affected families will be supported if they prefer not to engage with the media. This includes strategies for keeping the media separate from families while the emergency is ongoing and support for families that may experience unwanted media attention at their homes.

Appendix A: References

Albrecht, Steve. 2010. "Threat Assessment Teams: Workplace and School Violence Prevention." *FBI Law Enforcement Bulletin (February 2010)*. http://www.fbi.gov/stats-services/publications/law-enforcement-bulletin/february-2010/threat-assessment-teams

Blair, J. Pete and M. Hunter Martaindale. 2010. *United States Active Shooter Events from 2000 to 2010: Training and Equipment Implications*. San Marcos, TX: Texas State University. http://alerrt.org/files/research/ActiveShooterEvents.pdf

Calhoun, Frederick and Stephen Weston. 2003. *Contemporary Threat Management: A Practical Guide for Identifying, Assessing, and Managing Individuals of Violent Intent*. San Diego, CA: Specialized Training Services.

Cornell, Dewey. 2009. *Recommended Practices for Virginia College Threat Assessment*. Richmond, VA: Virginia Department of Criminal Justice Services. http://www.threatassessment.vt.edu/resources/tat_info/VArecommended_practices.pdf

Deisinger, Gene, et al. 2008. *The Handbook for Campus Threat Assessment and Management Teams*. Stoneham, MA: Applied Risk Management.

Federal Bureau of Investigation (FBI). 2002. *Workplace Violence: Issues in Response*. Quantico, VA: FBI. http://www.fbi.gov/stats-services/publications/workplace-violence

Federal Emergency Management Agency (FEMA). 2011. *A Whole Community Approach to Emergency Management: Principles, Themes, and Pathways for Action*. Washington, DC: FEMA. http://www.fema.gov/library/viewRecord.do?id=4941

> 2010. *Developing and Maintaining Emergency Operations Plans (Comprehensive Preparedness Guide [CPG] 101), Version 2.0*. Washington, DC: FEMA. http://www.fema.gov/plan

Fein, Robert, et al. 1995. *Threat Assessment: An Approach to Prevent Targeted Violence*. Washington, DC: U.S. Department of Justice. http://www.secretservice.gov/ntac/ntac_threat.pdf

Monahan, John, et al. 2001. *Rethinking Risk Assessment: The MacArthur Study of Mental Disorder and Violence*. New York, NY: Oxford University Press.

U.S. Department of Education, et al. 2013. *Guide for Developing High-quality School Emergency Operations Plans*. Washington, DC: U.S. Department of Education. http://rems.ed.gov

U.S. Department of Homeland Security (DHS). 2012. *Threat and Hazard Identification and Risk Assessment Guide (CPG 201)*. Washington, DC: DHS. http://www.fema.gov/plan

> 2012. *Homeland Security Advisory Council's Faith-based Security and Communications Advisory Committee Final Report*. Washington, DC: DHS. http://www.dhs.gov/xlibrary/assets/hsac/hsac-faith-based-security-and-communications-advisory-committee-final-report-may-2012.pdf

> 2011. *National Preparedness Goal*. Washington, DC: DHS. http://www.fema.gov/national-preparedness-goal

2008. *National Incident Management System.* Washington, DC: DHS. http://www.fema.gov/national-incident-management-system

2008. *Active Shooter: How to Respond.* Washington, DC: DHS. http://www.dhs.gov/xlibrary/assets/active_shooter_booklet.pdf

U.S. Secret Service and U.S. Department of Education. 2004. *The Final Report and Findings of the Safe School Initiative: Implications for the Prevention of School Attacks in the United States.* Washington, DC: U.S. Secret Service and U.S. Department of Education. http://www2.ed.gov/admins/lead/safety/preventingattacksreport.pdf

2002. *Threat Assessment in Schools: A Guide to Managing Threatening Situations and to Creating Safe School Climates.* Washington, DC: U.S. Secret Service and U.S. Department of Education. http://www.secretservice.gov/ntac/ssi_guide.pdf

U.S. Secret Service, et al. 2010. *Campus Attacks: Targeted Violence Affecting Institutions of Higher Education.* Washington, DC: U.S. Secret Service, U.S. Department of Education, and FBI. http://www2.ed.gov/admins/lead/safety/campus-attacks.pdf

Virginia Tech Review Panel. 2007. *Mass Shootings at Virginia Tech: Report of the Review Panel.* Richmond, VA: Virginia Tech Review Panel. http://www.governor.virginia.gov/tempContent/techPanelReport-docs/FullReport.pdf

Made in the USA
Middletown, DE
15 March 2018